Living in the United States

Its language, culture, and customs

★ ★ ★ ★ ★ ★ ★ ★ ★ ★ ★ ★

アメリカで暮らす

英語・文化・習慣

谷道 和子

Kazuko Tanimichi

三 恵 社

To students,

The purpose of this book is to help people who are going to live in the United States with both English and culture. Since the way people think, speak, and behave is deeply connected to their culture, understanding American culture is critical for learning English. This book will facilitate your stay in the United States and help you to carry out your work or study.

Concerning English, students can improve three skills (listening, speaking, and reading), vocabulary, and grammar in 'Survival English.' Therefore, the topics chosen are ones that meet students' needs to start their lives in America. One example is opening your account at a bank. This textbook familiarizes students with practical vocabulary. This will allow you to establish your life in America right after your arrival. Since using socially acceptable words is important in the United States, these expressions are shown first. Japanese people need to learn them before they leave since they have grown up in a mostly homogeneous society.

In listening and speaking, students are encouraged to listen to the English that people speak naturally in American society. This will make it easier for you to understand the natural spoken language. In order to improve your conversation skills, students are encouraged to use the English that they have learned for the means of communications.

Through reading articles, students are expected to understand the contents, the issues and cultures in America, and to develop their own ideas.

The important point of grammar instruction is the proper use of grammar, appropriate for the context. Students can learn the grammar of expressions that they need to use appropriately in real society. Another point is the grammar that Japanese students do not understand well or misunderstand. Students need to recognize their mistakes before they meet problems.

It is common sense that people should behave politely both in speech and attitude when they live overseas. However, people cannot avoid situations in which different cultures and customs clash when they leave their countries. As a result, things might not go well. Therefore, you need to have a certain amount of foreknowledge concerning American cultures and customs to avoid such unhappy situations. This text helps students understand American cultural issues.

I hope that this textbook will help students become familiar with practical English and American culture so that they can live in the United States. At the same time, I expect that students will improve their English for communication. Finally, I hope their life in the United States goes well even if they are busy in new places. I truly expect that their expectations of their stay in the United States will be fulfilled.

Kazuko Tanimichi

学習される皆さんへ

　このテキストは、これからアメリカに滞在される皆さんを、英語と文化、双方で助けるために作成されたものです。人々の考え方、話し方、振る舞いは、人々の文化と深く結びついているものであり、アメリカ文化を理解する事は、英語を学ぶために不可欠な事だからです。このテキストは、皆さんの、アメリカでの暮らしを容易にし、皆さんの学習や仕事を成功に導く事を助けるためのものです。

　英語に関しては、三つのスキル（リスニング、スピーキング、リーディング）、語彙、文法を、サバイバル英語において学ぶことが出来ます。従って、トピックスは、アメリカでの暮らしを始めるために不可欠な分野が選ばれています。一例として、銀行で口座を開く事が上げられます。語彙に関しては、実生活において是非必要とされる物を学ぶ事が出来ます。アメリカ到着後、直ちに、暮らしを確立する必要があるからです。アメリカ社会においては、社会で受け入れられている言葉を使う事が大切であり、その語彙は、最初に紹介されています。日本人は、ほぼ、単一民族からなる社会で成長していますので、出発前に学んでおく必要があります。

　リスニング、スピーキングにおいては、皆さんに、アメリカ社会で話されている自然の英語を聞いていただきます。アメリカで、皆さんに、実際の場面において、英語を理解していただく事を容易にするためです。会話力を上達させるために、このテキストにおいては、皆さんが、理解した英語を、コミュニケーションの手段として使っていただく事が期待されています。

　リーディングにおいては、皆さんには、課題とアメリカ文化についての主旨を理解し、自身の考えを深めていただく事が期待されます。

　文法においては、状況に合うように、適切に使うことが大切です。皆さんには、アメリカでの実生活において、文法を適切に使い表現する事を学んでいただきます。また、皆さんが、よく理解されていないか、あるいは、誤解されている文法を学んでいただきます。アメリカで、文法の不適切な使い方による問題を起こす前に、認識していただく必要があるのです。

　海外で暮らす時、言葉使い、態度において、礼儀正しくある事は当然の事です。しかし、異なる文化、習慣がぶつかる事態に遭遇する事を避ける事が出来ません。その結果、物事が、立ち行かなくなる事があります。そのような状況を避けるために、アメリカ文化と習慣について、事前に学ぶ必要があります。このテキストは、皆さんのアメリカ滞在を、文化面においても支えるためのものです。

　私は、皆さんが、このテキストを通して、アメリカで暮らすために、実践的な英語とその文化に理解を深められる事を望んでいます。同時に、皆さんが、コミュニケーションとしての英語力を高められる事を期待しています。最後に、このテキストを通して、皆さんの、アメリカでの新しい暮らしが、多忙なスケジュールにおいても、日々、前進するように願っています。皆さんの、アメリカ滞在目的が、実現される事を願ってやみません。

谷道 和子

CONTENTS

Grammar	Reading
Could; ask people with polite expressions	"Diverse people live in America":Reading about the diversity in America and the necessity of respecting people
Would like; the polite expression of want	"Check and signature" :Reading about the reason why people pay by check and the importance of your signature
The Distinguish the use of a/the	"Be safe: Protect yourself, Dorm, Don't hold back, Say facts and be direct, Some behavior acceptable in Japan violates the law in America"
Must Appropriate contexts where **must** is used	"An argument caused by the translation from the Japanese language" :English education based on translation, appropriate use of must
Could: the past tense of the modal verb **can** Does it mean past? The appropriate use of past, present, and future	"Issues of the medical insurance in America and Japanese people getting medication in the United States" : the background, culture, dentistry
Should; give advice	The analysis of cultural clash in a house, the solution for better life
Present perfect Using present perfect, create conversations	Studying overseas "Sharing a house with roommates": cultural differences, valuable experiences
The use of Much with noncount nouns The people in Vermont don't have much snow this winter.	"Driving in Vermont" :the beauty and rich nature, skiing, covered bridges, the development, comfortable life

Unit 1　Could you smoke in a smoking area?

1 CONVERSATION

Smoke Free

A ▶ **Listen and practice.** 🔘 CD-01

Listen to the conversations without looking at the textbook. Then answer the following questions.

Taro: It was a long flight, wasn't it? We are finally in America!

Yoko: Yes, we are!   Our new life starts from here. I'm excited!

Taro: Yes, we are going to become university students soon, here in the United States!

Yoko: Yes, we are!

(Taro starts smoking)

Waitress: Excuse me, sir? You are not allowed to smoke here. Could you smoke in a smoking area? Thank you.

Taro: Oh, I'm sorry. I didn't know that.

(Taro stops smoking)

Taro: But, Yoko, look at that behind you! It's written there on the wall: "Smoke Free."

Yoko: Taro. This means people who don't smoke are free from smokers' smoking. So smokers are not allowed to smoke here.

Taro: Really? I didn't know that!

Yoko: Now we are going to live in this country. We have to respect the people, habits, laws, manners, and cultures in this country.

Taro: Yes, definitely. This will make our studies here successful.

Yoko: Yes, it will! Besides, it will make our lives here comfortable.

Question

Question 1. Where does the conversation take place?

_____

Question 2. Is anyone allowed to smoke there?

_____

Question 3. What does "Smoke Free" mean?

_____

Question 4. What do people need to respect when they live in foreign countries?

_____

Question 5. Practice the conversation with your partners. Then switch roles.

B CD-02

Listen to the rest of the conversation. Find out how to get to a smoking area. Draw the picture based on the waitress's suggestions.

Taro: Excuse me? Could you show me where the smoking area is?

Waitress: Sure.

Taro: I need to refresh myself. Smoking is the best way to do that.

Waitress: Go down the hall this way. You'll see Exit B on your right. Turn left there. Go down the hall. And you'll see a café at the end of the hall. Right next to the café, on the right side, behind a vending machine, there is a hall.

Taro: Thank you.

Waitress: You're welcome.

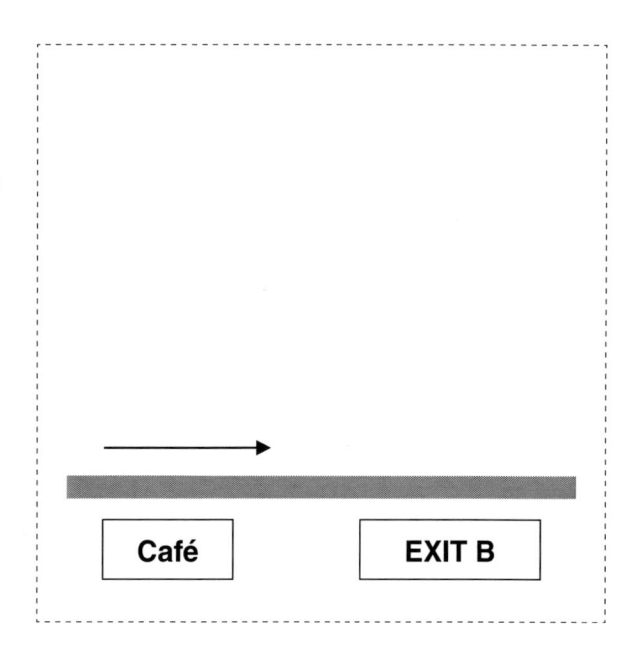

2 GRAMMAR FOCUS

Could you...?

When people ask someone for something, they usually use the polite expression, Could You...?

Using **could you**..., make polite question sentences in following situations.

a. You need to go shopping. Ask someone where the shopping mall is.

Excuse me. Could you tell me where the shopping mall is?

b. Your neighbor's TV sounds too noisy. This bothers you.

_____ (turn down)

c. You need a ride. Ask someone about it.

_____ (give me a ride)

d. Having dinner with friends, you'd like to eat salad. You need to ask someone to pass the salad bowl on the table to you.

_____ (pass something to me)

3 READING

Diverse people live in America.

"Not black or white, this is the United States." As a candidate for the future President of the United States, Barack Obama appealed the people one of political value in his election campaign. The value is that diverse people and things should be united in one country under the name, "the United States of America." He persuaded people that diverse people should respect each other in order to be united within a country.

Since Japan is a mostly homogeneous country, the Japanese people need to learn about racial issues and diversity in America before they leave Japan. First of all, some vocabulary which we are familiar with and use in Japan is unacceptable in the United States. For example, American people call the people whose ancestors have come from Japan "Japanese-Americans," and people whose ancestors have come from Africa "African-Americans." The expression, "African- American," is acceptable, while other expressions or words we are unconsciously using, like Black people or Negro, to denote African-Americans is often unacceptable in America. The acceptable expression for the people who have originally lived in the country is Native Americans, not Indians. The people who came from Latin-America are called Hispanic. Caucasian is another expression for White people. When people use some vocabulary concerning race, they use the one which is the most acceptable.

American people have diverse differences in cultures, languages, religions, customs, and habits. Recognizing these differences, American people try to mutually respect their different backgrounds in order to be united as one country. If people did not respect the diverse differences among each other, America would be divided. Children and students are taught about diversity and respecting differences among each other at school. American people think of diversity as a treasure. Diverse people have brought the country diverse talents.

Japanese people need to recognize racial diversity in the United States and respect differences in order to live in America. Having the spirit to respect each other make them choose appropriate words and polite attitude against people. When people respect each other, they are united, even though they are foreigners, with the people in the United States.

Connect the words and the definitions with a line. Then practice asking and answering the questions with a partner.

Who is …?	**She/he is the person who/whose …**
1. Native American	**a.** ancestor came from Latin America
2. African- American	**b.** belongs to the race that has white skin
3. Hispanic	**c.** ancestor originally came from Japan
4. Japanese- American	**d.** ancestor originally came from Africa
5. Caucasian	**e.** has originally been living in North America

Write some important things that Japanese people need to keep in minds when they live in America.

1. _____

2. _____

Unit 2 — I'd like to open an account here.

Could you show me your student ID?

ABC BANK

1 WORD POWER

Match the words with their definitions.

a. account

b. check book

c. checking account

d. savings account

e. withdraw

f. deposit

g. save

1. To add money to a bank account

2. To take out your money from a bank

3. An arrangement that you have with a bank to save or withdraw money

4. The account that you can take money out of at any time

5. A small book which your bank gives you. With your signature, you can use it to directly transfer money to another person or business.

6. The money that is put into a bank to open your account

7. The account that accumulates interest

2 CONVERSATION

A Listen and practice. 🔘 CD-03

Listen to the following conversation and answer the questions.

Clerk: Hi. May I help you?

Yoko: Yes. I'd like to open an account here. I'm a student from Japan.

Clerk: Sure. Have a seat. Could you show me your student ID?

Yoko: My student ID?

Clerk: Yes. You should have a student ID issued by your college. We need your ID to open your account. The card that identifies you.

Yoko: I'm sorry. I don't have a student ID yet. I arrived here yesterday.

Clerk: Hmm. Do you have your passport?

Yoko: Yes, I have my passport. Here you are.

Clerk: Thanks. Could you write down your name, birth date, current address, and phone number on this sheet? And we need your signature here.

Yoko: Sure. By the way, I don't have much money with me right now.

Clerk: No problem. If you can deposit any amount greater than $5 that would be fine.

Yoko: Sure. Can I deposit $50 by traveler's check?

Clerk: Sure. You have now opened your account here. This is your account number.

Yoko: Thank you. My mother is going to send me money from my account at a bank in Japan.

Clerk: You need to notify the bank in Japan of your account number here and our bank code.

Yoko: Sure, I will. I'll send the information to Japan today.

******

Clerk: Ma'am, We will mail you a statement, which is a summary of the total deposits into and spending from each account, once a month. Please check it. You have two accounts. One is a checking account. You can withdraw money from it at any time. The other account is a savings account. You can withdraw money from it only a few times a month. Instead, it will accumulate interest. Currently, the interest rate in this country is 3% per year. This is a check book. When you would like to make a payment using a check, you need to write down the amount of money here and then sign your name here. OK? You are all set. Do you have any questions?

Debit card

Nowadays, many banks recommend that you have a debit card. The merit of having a debit card is that you can use it to make purchases and it will withdraw money directly from your account. You don't need to write out a check. Since this doesn't take a lot of time, people don't wait in long lines at the cash registers of shopping malls. Whether or not you have a debit card is your decision.

Question 1. Where does the conversation take place?

_____

Question 2. What kind of identification did she show to the clerk to open her account?

_____

Question 3. What did she deposit to open her account?

_____

Question 4. What is the bank going to mail her once a month?

_____

Question 5. How can Yoko use her check book?

_____

B ▶ **Practice the conversations with your partner.**

3 READING

Check and signature

1) In the United States, people don't carry a lot of money in cash when they go out. They usually carry around thirty dollars in cash. Having only a small amount of cash saves them from losing money in the event that their wallet is lost or stolen.

2) You might think that you can't buy anything with thirty dollars. Don't worry. People always carry check books issued by their banks. They use checks when they go shopping, to pay their rent, and to pay their school tuitions. Therefore, it is important that they should always have enough money in their bank account for the amount they have used in a check and debit card.

3) Personal stamps, _hanko_, are not used in the United States. Instead, a person's signature is used. Before people sign their names on documents, they ask themselves what their signature will be used for. Writing their name on a document forms a contract that they must uphold. Therefore, people are especially cautious when signing their name for matters concerning money. People make sure that the person they are paying money to and the amount are correct and then they sign their names on documents. The money signed by you is withdrawn from your account.

A

Read the article. Then write the number of each paragraph next to its main idea.

a. ____ People are careful when signing their name on documents.

b. ____ People need to keep money in their accounts for the payments they have made.

c. ____ People carry only a small amount of money with them in case they lose their wallet.

B

Write two important things to remember when you sign a document.

a. _____

b. _____

4 GRAMMAR FOCUS

Using **would like to**, ask and answer this question with your partner. Then, report your partner's answer to the class.

Question: What would you like to do in the United States?

Example:
A: What would you like to do in the United States?
B: I'd like to visit Yellowstone National Park in Wyoming.
A: She wants to visit Yellowstone National Park in Wyoming.

Unit 3 International students need to attend orientation.

1 WORD POWER

Fill in each blank with the appropriate word below in its appropriate form.

credit	tuition	semester	administration office

1. When you need to contact a college, you should call the (   ).

2. Usually, the school year of universities in the United States consists of two or three (   ).

3. Full time students must take a minimum of twelve (   ) in each semester at this college.

4. Students must pay their (   ) at the beginning of each semester.

2 LISTENING

The procedures before school starts.

Hi, Yoko!
Welcome to our university.

Listen to the conversation and answer the questions.

Pauline: Good morning. This is the administration office, Pauline speaking.

Yoko: This is Yoko Sato speaking. I'm a new student from Japan. I just arrived here yesterday.

Pauline: Hi, Yoko! Welcome to our university.

Yoko: Hi. I need to meet with Ms. William at your office.

Pauline: Great, that's me. Do you know where my office is?

Yoko: Yes, I know the location. It's in the Parentis Hall, on the left side from the east entrance, right?

Pauline: Right. Please bring your passport and the document that I have sent you when you come.

Yoko: Yes, I will. See you there.

Question 1. Where did Yoko call?

_____

Question 2. What does she need to bring when she meets Pauline?

_____

🔘 CD-05

(At the administration office)

Pauline: Yoko, this is your identification card, issued by this school. We call it a "student ID". This identifies who you are. You always have to carry it while you are here. Please don't lose it.

Yoko: No, I won't.

Pauline: Right. As you know, there is an orientation at Willers Hall, in the afternoon, at 1:30. International students must attend it. Please listen to the teacher's explanation carefully. It will help your life as a student here.

Yoko: I see. I will listen to it carefully.

Pauline: Good. Before the orientation, you will need to meet your adviser. You must take a minimum of twelve credits each semester.

Yoko: Twelve credits? I see. I am glad that this college has accepted me as a student, but I worry if I'll be able to understand what professors say in classes.

Pauline: I see.

Yoko: I arrived here yesterday, but I've already been in some environments where I couldn't understand what Americans were saying. I'm going to study with American classmates who have been speaking English since they were born. I'm afraid that I won't be able to follow my classes because I'm not a native speaker.

Pauline: Don't worry! Talk about this with your adviser. She will help you.

Yoko: Okay.

Pauline: This college provides some English courses for international students, like you, but you cannot receive credit from those classes.

Yoko: I see.

Pauline: But taking English courses for international students will help you to understand the content of classes at this college. Besides, you will be comfortable there. Your adviser will help you with issues concerning your studies. When you meet with your adviser, you need to decide what classes you are going to take. If there are any questions about the tuition bill, you can visit the registrar's office. Do you have any questions?

Yoko: No, thank you for your help. I'll go to meet my adviser.

Pauline: Good luck with your studies. Have a nice day.

Yoko: Thank you. You, too.

Question 3. What is a student ID?

_____

Question 4. Where is the orientation held? Who needs to attend the orientation? Why do you think they need to attend it?

_____

Question 5. What is Yoko's concern with her classes right now?

_____

Question 6. Can students receive credit for taking the English classes for international students?

_____

Question 7. Discuss Pauline's point of view concerning Yoko taking the English classes.

_____

Question 8. Where is Yoko going once she leaves Pauline's office? State her schedule in chronological order.

_____

B▶ Practice the conversations with your partner.

While reading each article, think about what is necessary to safely enjoy American life. Then, answer each question.

Be safe: Protect yourself.

When you go out, tell someone where you are going and who you will be with before you leave. In case something happens to you, the information you have left with them might become the clue to finding you.

Don't go out late at night and in the early morning alone. While studying in a foreign country far away from your parents, you might feel lonely and want to go out for a cup of coffee downtown even if it is late at night. This can be dangerous. Please keep in mind that you are not in Tokyo.

When studying at the college library until late at night, ask the escort service of your college to go back home with you or go back home with a friend whom you can trust. Don't walk alone in the late evening even if it is only a short distance from your campus.

Don't go to places where no one is seen even if it is inside a school building and daytime.

Don't explore places that Americans say not to go to even if you are interested in visiting there. Keep in mind that you are not in Japan.

Question 1. Compare the situations you encounter in Tokyo, what do you need to do to protect yourself while in the United States? Discuss with your group.

Dorm

There is no *mon-gen,* curfew, at the dormitories of colleges in the United States. American university students already have the right to vote. Who needs to control them with a curfew?

The people who work in dorms are students except for a couple of officers. They check those who enter and exit the dorm. Friends of a student who lives in a dorm can visit her or him at the dorm. The person who works at the reception of the dorm makes sure that the visitors check in and check out.

The basic rules of a dorm are that students should not bother other students or break the furniture. Students who violate the rules might be ordered to leave or charged a fine. The rules are totally different from the type of the dorm that Japanese parents would believe to be secure for their sons and daughters.

Since there are no strict rules that control and limit students' private life or behaviors, students need to make decisions by themselves concerning their actions and safety. This forces students to discipline themselves and become mature.

Question 2. Why do Japanese parents think that their children will be safe when they live in dorms?

_____

Question 3. Who is in charge of students' safety?

_____

Don't hold back.

Suppose you are studying while your roommate who lives in another room is listening to music in her room. The music bothers you when you study. You'd like to ask her to turn down the sound, but you are afraid of making her angry. This happens every day, and you hold in your feelings. As a result, your frustration has been accumulating day by day. The solution is that you shouldn't hold back and tell her the problem frankly.

Here is my experience. I was in this situation, and one day I finally asked my roommate, "Could you turn down the music? I'm studying." Showing her surprise on her face, she said, "I'm sorry. I didn't know that! I must have bothered you!" She immediately turned down the music and apologized to me. I thought, "What was the point of holding back my feelings for so many days?" My anger towards her had accumulated, and my studies hadn't gone well. I was unhappy for many days because I held back my feelings.

The solution came from only one sentence that I asked her. Holding back your true feelings doesn't lead to any good solution. In general, Americans value individual life, and at a same time they respect the lives of others, too.

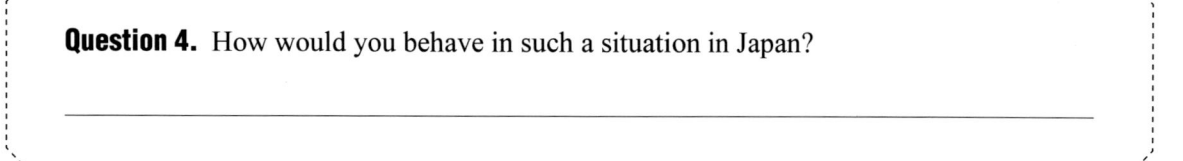

> **Question 4.** How would you behave in such a situation in Japan?
>
> _____

Say facts and be direct.

Japanese people prefer to use indirect speech. They feel that indirect expressions are more polite than direct expressions, especially for important things. This often makes Americans frustrated and causes misunderstandings between Americans and Japanese people.

While listening to the polite explanations of a Japanese person, Americans often ask Japanese people, "What's your point?" When they hear this question, Japanese people need to make their explanation clear. Japanese indirect speech is often ambiguous for Americans.

Even in advertisements of hamburgers on TV in the United States, prices are written and announced directly and clearly with the pictures at first. When I saw this, I was shocked. I felt the American way of advertising was too straightforward and, therefore, not sophisticated. Soon I realized that advertisements that come with the price allow the audience to decide whether they will purchase it or not. These advertisements are helpful because they give clear information to the audience. A person's decision about buying something is deeply related to its price.

> **Question 5.** Do you think you speak your point of view clearly in Japan? Describe situations in which you hesitate to use direct speech.
>
> _____
>
> **Question 6.** What would you think if American advertisements were broadcasted on TV in Japan?
>
> _____

Some behavior acceptable in Japan violates the law in America.

There are laws in each country, and these laws govern the people in that country. When people live in a foreign country, they must respect the laws where they live. However, some behavior which is acceptable in their home country might be illegal in a different county. Because of this, foreigners might cause serious problems if they are ignorant. One example is that the American laws relating to alcohol are quite different from those of Japan. Therefore, Japanese people need to have some basic prior knowledge regarding the American laws which relate to alcohol.

In the United States, people cannot drink alcoholic beverages until they become 21 years old. Besides, young people are asked to show their ID when they go to liquor shop to buy beer. Meanwhile, all Japanese people whether they are teens or seniors can buy cold beer and other alcoholic beverages at vending machines anywhere at any time all over Japan. This means that we can enjoy cold beer whenever we want. Although teens drinking alcoholic beverages is illegal in Japan, we seldom hear that drinking teens cause problems or commit a crime. Anyhow, people have a generous attitude regarding the dealing of alcoholic beverages and drunken peoples' behaviors in Japan.

When I arrived at the dorm of my college in Indiana, I really wanted to drink a can of cold beer. After studying hard for many years to get the permission to study at the college and long flight, I finally arrived there. I expected to celebrate my efforts and my future studies with a can of cold beer. However, I couldn't find a vending machine to buy beer anywhere around the campus. I felt that life in America was inconvenient. The following day, someone told me that it was a forty-minute-walk to get to the closest liquor shop. When I arrived there, the owner of the liquor shop asked me to show him my ID. While showing my passport to him, I realized that Japan is a special society regarding the dealing of alcoholic beverages. Although I wanted to buy a can of cold beer, I had to buy a dozen cans of beer, which were not cooled. This form of celebration on my second day in America with lukewarm beer dissatisfied me. If I had been in Japan, I would have celebrated on the night of my arrival with cold beer.

Another totally different aspect of the law in some states in America from that of Japan relates to when men date women. In some states, drunk women are protected by the law. This means that a drunk woman who engages in sexual acts with a man can accuse him for law suits after the dating even if she has wanted it.

In this case, the man can't win the law suit because she was drunk. This happens even if she only had a glass of wine. A professor of psychology at Saint Michael's College in Vermont persuaded international students during orientation not to cause problems because of their ignorance of the law in Vermont. Although a woman might have given her consent, men have to remember that the law might protect women who have consumed alcohol.

As you have read, the American laws concerning alcohol are very strict. Therefore, while you are living in the United States, you need to keep in mind that the laws in the United States are different from those of Japan. Good luck! You will not be sued by a person in the United States.

Question 7. Describe some important points for living in the United States without violating the law.

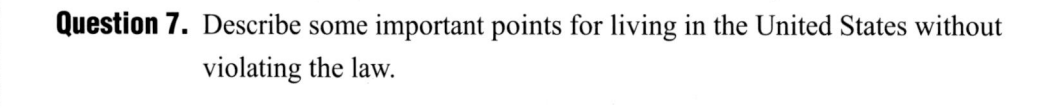

4 GRAMMAR FOCUS

Think about the use of articles in the two conversations below.

    A: I'd like to buy <u>a kerosene</u> heater.

    B: Go to XYZ mart! They are on sell right now.

    A: Really? I'll definitely buy it over there.

****

    A: I'd like to buy <u>the kerosene</u> heater.

    B: This one? Go to the office and ask the boss. I'm not sure if he will sell it to you. It is installed in this room.

> The grammar rule for the definite article, **the**: when speakers and listeners can mutually understand what is being referred to, the definite article, **the**, is used.

1

Suppose you and your partner are in the room of the picture below. Using the items in the picture, create conversations with your partner. You need to distinguish between the use of the articles **a/an** and **the** in your conversations.

Conversation

A: I need to call my mom.   Can I use (   ) phone?

B: Sure, please.

A: Thanks.

2

Talk about things and situations that your partner does not know.

Conversation

A: I bought (   ) sweater for my mother yesterday.

B: Oh, did you?

A: But the problem is that she doesn't like (   ) color.   I bought a pink one.

B: You should go to (   ) store with your mother and have her chose whatever she likes.

Unit 4 — Could you clean the kitchen after you cook?

1 CONVERSATION

A Japanese student says, "You *must* clean the kitchen after you use it."

 A CD-06

Listen to the following conversation. Then answer the questions.

Yoko's landlady, Yoko, and a male student, Saeed, from an Islamic country are sharing a kitchen in a house. Saeed always leaves his dishes and pans around the sink after he cooks. Their landlady always tells Yoko to keep the kitchen clean. One morning, Yoko comes into the kitchen to cook.

Yoko: Again!? Our kitchen is so messy. Saeed never cleans the kitchen after he cooks. I need to talk about it to him. Our landlady always thinks I'm the one who leaves the kitchen a mess.

(Saeed walks through the kitchen to go to school.)

Saeed: Hi! Yoko. Good morning.
 Yoko: Good morning. Saeed, I need to talk to you for a minute.
Saeed: Sorry, I'm in a hurry. My class starts soon.
 Yoko: Oh, I know you are in a hurry, but you *must* clean the kitchen after you use it!
Saeed: I *must*? I'll wash them after my class. I don't have time to wash them right now. It's a small thing. Why are you so angry?
 Yoko: It's common sense to wash the dishes after you cook. Three people share a kitchen. Besides, our landlady always tells me to clean the kitchen. She is angry at me because you leave the kitchen a mess.
Saeed: I just leave my dishes for a while. Why do you say I *must* clean the kitchen? Do you have a right to say that? I gotta go!

Question 1. Why did Yoko tell Saeed to wash the dishes after he uses the kitchen?

_____

Question 2. Why do you think Saeed is so angry?

_____

Question 3. What's wrong with her expression? "You *must* clean the kitchen after you use it!" Why did she use this expression?

_____

Question 4. What kind of expressions should Yoko have used to Saeed? Answer appropriate expressions in this situation.

1. _____

2. _____

3. _____

B Practice the conversations with your partner.

2 READING

Read the essay. Then answer the questions.

An argument caused by the translation from the Japanese language.

We, the Japanese people, have learned English at school through Grammar-Translation Method (GTM) since the Meiji era. The theory of GTM is that the grammar rule is explicit. Students memorize vocabulary based on translations. Then they translate English to Japanese based on the grammar rule to understand readings. The method was used in European countries to learn Latin, a dead language. No one used Latin as the means for communication. Scholars used the GTM to read Latin archives. The Japanese Education Ministry used the method in the English education as European countries had used for the education of Latin.

Since the Japanese people have learned English through Grammar-Translation Method, they use the method to speak English, too. They translate the Japanese language to English based on the grammar rule that they have learned at school. The Japanese expression, *tukatta ato wa* *katazukenake<u>nebanaranai</u>*, is a formal expression in the Japanese language. Moreover, having manners among the people is explicit to keep the harmony in the Japanese society. Therefore, it is explicit that people clean the kitchen for the next person when they share it with other people. The appropriate English vocabulary of the Japanese language, *nebanaranai*, is *must*. Therefore, the Japanese people translate the expression, *tukatta ato wa katazukenake<u>nebanaranai</u>*, to the expression of English, You *must* clean the kitchen after you use it. They think that the expression is appropriate both grammatically and socially in English.

However, Yoko's conversation, you *must* clean the kitchen after you use it, has caused the anger of her roommate. This means that speaking English based on translation from Japanese to English is problematic. The Japanese students should have been taught appropriate contexts in which the auxiliary, *must*, is used and practiced it as the means for communication. English study based on translation is no problem on the exams in Japan. However, this caused a problem in a kitchen in America. Yoko had to explain to Saeed that she didn't have any intension to offend him. Furthermore, she told him that the expression was the English that she had learned in Japan.

By the way, what's wrong with the expression, you *must* clean the kitchen? The answer is that people in the United States don't use *must* in their daily conversation. We, the Japanese people, need to learn the appropriate contexts in which American people use *must*. According to Azar, following are four contexts that American people use the auxiliary, must. An example sentence is written for each. **Necessity, there is no other choice:** All applicants must take an entrance exam (Azar p 75). **Law:** People must have passports to go abroad. **Prohibition:** You must not tell anyone my secret. Do you promise? (Azar p 76) **Strong degree of certainty, 95% sure:** John isn't in class. He must be sick (Azar p 89). As you see, the auxiliary verb, must, has a strong meaning. Therefore, the Japanese people need to keep the idea that American people do not use the auxiliary verb, must, in daily English. Using English based on translation causes problems. We, Japanese people, must make sure of the context in which we translate the Japanese word, *nebanaranai*, to English in communication.

When the use of the auxiliary, must, is inappropriate in English, what kind of expressions should we use? The appropriate expressions for "You *must* clean the kitchen after you use it" are following: Could you clean the kitchen after you use it?; You need to clean the kitchen after you use it; You have to clean the kitchen after you use it; or, Can I ask you to clean the kitchen after you use it? These are acceptable expressions in America.

What I can make sure is the right use of the auxiliary verb, must, doesn't hurt people and doesn't cause their angers against you.

Question 1. Explain one of the teaching methods of English, the Grammar-Translation Method.

_____

Question 2. Explain why people in Europe used the Grammar-Translation Method.

_____

Question 3. Tell the reasons why Yoko told her roommate, Saeed, "You must clean the kitchen after you use it."

a. _____

b. _____

Question 4. What should Yoko have been taught concerning the auxiliary, must, in the English class in Japan?

a. _____

b. _____

3 GRAMMAR FOCUS

A

Make sure whether the context in which 'must' is used is appropriate in each sentence. Write 'a' if the context that 'must' is used is appropriate and 'i' if the use of the context is inappropriate in each parenthesis. Then using other auxiliaries, write correct expressions when the answer is inappropriate. There might be multiple expressions.

a. (   ) Students <u>must</u> study.

b. (   ) Students <u>must</u> play sports.

c. (   ) People <u>must</u> have a passport to go abroad.

d. (   ) A three-year-old girl is crying without any specific reason. Her father said, "She is weary. She <u>must</u> be sleepy."

e (   ) President Obama said, "All Americans <u>must</u> have medical insurance."

f. (   ) Recently, the number of children is decreasing. Men <u>must</u> do chores and take care of their children at home so that women will want to have more children.

g. (   ) Following is a conversation between a customer, a young man, and a liquor shop owner. "I am 21 years old. I'd like to buy beer." " You <u>must</u> show me your identification."

h. (   ) The scenery of Key West in Florida is so nice, so you <u>must</u> visit there when you travel to Florida.

B

Complete the sentences with your own words. They need to be grammatically and socially acceptable.

(example answers)

a. You must not…   *You must not smoke here.*

b. Children don't have to…   *Children don't have to go to school on Sunday.*

c. Children need to…

d. Parents must…

e I have to…

f. The pharmacist said, "You must…

(take two pills)

C

Imagine the feeling of the speaker who says, "Must you smoke here?"

Unit 5 Can I make an appointment with a doctor?

1 CONVERSATION

A▶ Can I make an appointment with a doctor? 🔊 CD-07

Listen to the conversation and answer the questions below. Then practice it with your partner.

Can I make an appointment with a doctor?

Ma'am, I need to make sure if you have medical insurance.

Receptionist:	Good morning. This is Dr. Caldwell's office. May I help you?
Yoko:	Yes. This is Yoko Sato speaking. Can I make an appointment with a doctor?
Receptionist:	Sure.
Yoko:	I just arrived in the United States. I have a high fever.
Receptionist:	That's too bad.
Yoko:	Could you tell me where the office is?
Receptionist:	Sure, it's on Marquette Avenue, the second floor of ABC building.
Yoko:	Where?
Receptionist:	194 Marquette Avenue, the second floor of ABC building. Could you tell me about your medical insurance?
Yoko:	What did you say? I am asking you where your office is. I am in a serious condition right now.
Receptionist:	We need to identify who you are.
Yoko:	How can I get there? I'd like to see a doctor as soon as possible.
Receptionist:	Ma'am, I need to make sure you have medical insurance.
Yoko:	I can't understand what you said. I'd like to make an appointment with a doctor.
Receptionist:	Ma'am, there are many doctors around here. If you cannot answer my question, you should go to another doctor's office. I need to hang up this phone.

Yoko: Medical insurance? Please, wait. Yes, I have a medical insurance issued in Japan. This covers all medical fees.

Receptionist: I see. Please come.

Question 1. Why do you think that the receptionist said that she would hang up the phone?

Question 2. Yoko gave some personal information to the receptionist to make an appointment with a doctor. Which information do you think that Yoko should have given to the receptionist at first?

Question 3. Yoko used the word **Japan** in her conversation. How do you think the word works in this context?

B What seems to be your problem?

Match the words and the definitions.

What does ...mean?	**It means....**
1. fever	**a.** an infectious disease which is like a cold
2. the flu	**b.** a pain in your throat
3. headache	**c.** the sound of air pushed from the throat
4. cough	**d.** the pain you feel in your head
5. sore throat	**e.** high body temperature

🔊 CD-08

Listen to the conversation and answer the questions. Then practice the conversation with your partner.

(at a consulting room)

Doctor: Hi. I'm Dr. Caldwell, nice to meet you. What seems to be your problem?

Yoko: I've caught a cold.

Doctor: Please tell me your symptoms.

Yoko: I have a fever and a headache. Also, I can't stop my coughing. I've been coughing all day long.

Doctor: Your temperature is 101 degrees Fahrenheit.

Yoko: 101 degrees!?

Doctor: You have a fever, but it's not so high.

Yoko: I feel terrible.

Doctor: You need to get some rest.

Yoko: Could you prescribe medicine for me? I have an exam tomorrow. I have to study.

Doctor: You've caught a cold. There is no medicine that works for a cold. Wash your hands and take a shower. Eat soup and drink orange juice.

Yoko: Is that all?

Doctor: That's the best way to treat your sickness.

Question 1. What symptoms does Yoko have?

_____

Question 2. How high is the temperature 101 degree Fahrenheit in Celsius?

_____

Question 3. What did Yoko want the doctor to do?

_____

Question 4. Why doesn't the doctor prescribe medicine for her?

_____

Question 5. What did the doctor tell Yoko to recover from the cold? Then explain the reason for each.

1. *Wash hands: to get rid of the germs* _____

2. _____

3. _____

4. _____

5. _____

2 WORD POWER

A▶ Organs

Fill in each blank with an appropriate word.

1. lung **2.** liver

3. kidney **4.** heart

5. stomach **6.** large intestine

7. bladder **8.** small intestine

(a.　　　) (e.　　　)
(b.　　　) (f.　　　)
(c.　　　) (g.　　　)
(d.　　　) (h.　　　)

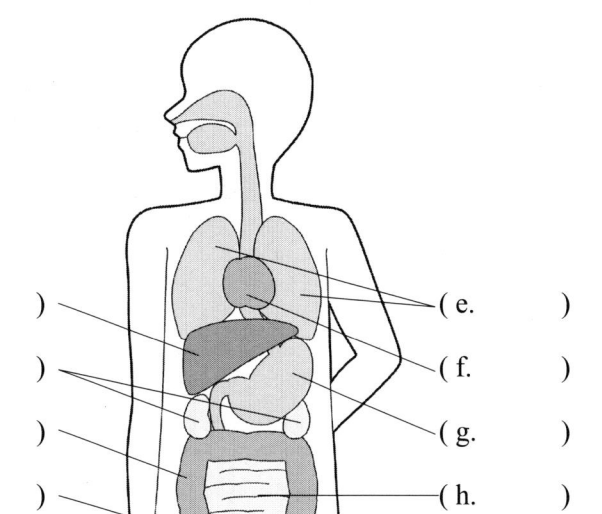

B▶ Terms related to medicine and illness

Match the word and the definition

1. appetite

2. bowel movement

3. sneeze

4. allergy

5. virus

6. urine

7. vomit

8. swelling

9. diarrhea

10. infect

a. a small living thing that causes infectious disease

b. a desire for food

c. a movement getting rid of solid waste from the human body

d. food that has come up from your stomach because of your illness

e. when a part of your body is bigger than usual

f. the liquid waste that comes out of your bladder

g. when air suddenly comes out of your nose and mouth

h. the illness caused by eating certain foods or touching certain things

i. the condition in which your stool is in liquid form

j. to give someone a disease

C 🔘 CD-09

Fill in each blank with an appropriate word from the exercise B. You need to change the form of some words. Then practice the listening and speaking of each expression.

a. Patient: "I have a fever, and I have been coughing all day long." "Because of this, I have a pain in my throat."

Doctor: "Your throat is red and (1.   )." "Can you eat?"

Patient: "No, I don't have a good (2.   )."

b. I am (3.   ) to pollen. I have a problem in my nose. I'm (4.   ) all day long.

c. I might have eaten something wrong. I am (5.   ) and have (6.   ), so I need to go to the bathroom so often.

d. A doctor said to a patient, "You've got the flu. It's an (7.   ) disease, so you need to stay home."

③ ROLE PLAY

Practice explaining the symptoms below to a doctor with your partner. Switch roles.

A

Doctor: Please tell me the symptoms.
Patient: I have pain in my belly.
Doctor: When did it start?
Patient: Yesterday. It started yesterday night. And...
Doctor:

B

Doctor:
Patient:
Doctor:
Patient:
Doctor:
Patient:

tissue   chicken soup

Doctor:

Patient:

Doctor:

Patient:

Doctor:

Patient:

4 READING

Issues of Medical Insurance and Japanese People Getting Medication in the United States.

Read the essay. Then answer the questions.

1)   In the United States, the government does not provide everyone with medical insurance. Each person or family has a contract with an insurance company for medical care. People who are hired by companies, for example, are often provided their medical insurance through their companies. Therefore, people who do not have jobs or people whose income is low have difficulty getting medicine even if they are in serious conditions. The reason is that poor people cannot afford to buy medical insurances by themselves. Even worse, insurance companies sometimes do not compensate for malignant diseases and terminal care. The reason is because the medical cost is extremely high and insurance companies do not want to pay. This means poor people, elderly people, people who have serious diseases, and those people who really need medical care have difficulty getting access to medication.

2)   One of the major policy attempts by former president Bill Clinton was to legislate Congress to establish Medicare and Medicaid in the United States and provide medical insurance for every American. He convinced the American people that doctors should decide what treatment patients get. He said, "It is doctors' decisions but not insurance companies." Both the president and his wife, Hillary, were enthusiastic about Medicare. However, they failed. One of the main reasons was that the American people were afraid of paying more money for their medical insurance. The second reason was that supporting oneself, even in regards to medical care, is part of American culture and tradition. Therefore, many people feel that the government establishing the policy in medical insurance is too big a change for the people.

3)   After the Bush administration, President Obama worked for the medical insurance in 2013. In June 2015, the Supreme Court ruled that the government's subsidies for Health Care were legal.

Because of this, sixteen million out of fifty million people who had not had medical insurance could buy it (Kawai June 26th). However, many people still do not have medical insurance. Moreover, many Americans are unhappy with the new law.

4) Before I studied in the United States, the people in Japan had said that people should get dental treatment in Japan before they leave. This idea is not true. One day in the United States, I felt the filling of one of my teeth had fallen on my tongue. I made an appointment with a dentist. What I worried about was the fee since I did not have medical insurance for dentistry. I told the dentist that I was going back home in summer. He explained that he would give me a temporary treatment. He refilled the cave of my tooth with the filling. Then he wrote the explanation of his treatment with the picture of the tooth, and then he told me to show the paper to my dentist in Japan. The money that the dentist charged me was $50 in 1995. Although the doctor told me the treatment was a temporary one, I did not have to go to a dentist for many years. I was satisfied with the treatment, and his kind attitude warms my heart even to this day.

5) One of my friends was getting dental treatment for all of her bad teeth while she was in the United States. The reason was that she was able to get better treatment for a lower fee than in Japan. Our medical insurance in Japan covers the fee for the white covers only for front teeth. If we get the treatment on the white cover on the teeth other than front teeth, the fee is much higher in Japan than that of the United States. She was happy with her beautiful teeth, the treatment that her American dentist had done, and the price.

6) I thought one of the reasons that Japanese people recommend that we get dental treatment before we leave was that they had gotten dental treatment when one dollar was worth three hundred and sixty yen. Secondly, since they couldn't speak English well, they had difficulty communicating with American dentists. Because of their unsatisfactory experiences, their advice is still taken by people in Japan.

7) Another medical example in America is that my Japanese friend who married an American delivered a baby at a hospital in Milwaukee. She told me that she was hospitalized only for forty eight hours. Insurance companies do not cover more days than that. Her husband was taking care of her. In Japan, women are usually hospitalized for a week after giving birth. Then women go back their parents' home for a month to recover from their deliveries. I analyzed that the difference in culture and insurance between Japan and the United States caused the difference in the length of time of hospitalization in delivery.

8) When you live in the United States, I recommend that you buy the medical insurance issued in Japan which covers all medical fees. Then you do not have to worry at all about paying medical fees in the United States. What you need is to study natural English which is used in American society so that you could communicate with American doctors.

A

Write the number of the paragraph where you find each answer.

( ) **a.** People in Japan suggest that those going to foreign countries should get dental treatment before they leave.

( ) **b.** Japanese medical insurance does not cover the fee for treatment of white cover to teeth except front teeth.

( ) **c.** A Japanese girl decided to treat all of her bad teeth in America before she left for Japan.

( ) **d.** President Bill Clinton was enthusiastic about providing medical insurance to all of the Americans.

( ) **e.** Some poor Americans have hardly any access to medical treatment.

( ) **f.** The time length of the hospitalization for baby delivery in America is much shorter than Japan.

B

Answer the questions.

1. Why do lower income people have difficulty getting medication in the U.S?

Because poor people cannot afford to buy medical insurance

2. Why do insurance companies sometimes not compensate for terminal care?

_____

3. Why did former president Bill Clinton say that doctors should make decision for the medical treatment that patients need?

_____

4. Why did Bill Clinton fail to establish the medical insurance system for all Americans?

1. _____

2. _____

3. _____

5. Why do women who give birth have to leave the hospital in 48 hours?

_____

6. Why did a Japanese student make a decision to treat her teeth while she was in the U.S?

1. _____

2. _____

3. _____

7. Why does the author oppose the peoples' advice about getting dental treatment before they leave Japan?

_____

_____

C Group work

Talk about the medicine in the United States. What impresses you the most?

5 GRAMMAR FOCUS

A

Write the tense of each sentence in the parenthesis. Then, if the sentence is grammatically correct, write (c) in the parenthesis. If it is incorrect, write (i).

	tense	i/c
1. I could run fast when I was a child.	( )	( )
2. I could run fast the day before yesterday.	( )	( )
3 I couldn't run fast the day before yesterday.	( )	( )
4. I was able to run fast last week.	( )	( )
5. I could speak English fluently if I study everyday.	( )	( )
6. Where is Jessica? She could be at home.	( )	( )

Explanation: **could** refers to ability which occurs over a long duration in past in affirmative sentences (1). People do not use **could** to show the ability in a particular time in past in affirmative sentences (2). They use **be able to** instead (4)(Azar p109). However, the negative form, couldn't, is used in a particular time in past (3). People use **could** to show the possibility in a future or present in affirmative sentences. (5, 6)(Azar p87).

B

Fill in each blank with *can't*, *could*, *couldn't*, or *was able to*, appropriately.

1. In the United States, many people, especially poor people, (   ) get medication because
they (   ) afford to buy medical insurance. Former president Bill Clinton pushed for a
medical insurance system so that all of the American people (   ) get medical insurance.

2. I have been studying for the TOEFL for a year. I (   ) get a score of 550 in the last exam.
I (   ) study in America if I want. My dream has come.

C Group work

Remember when you were young. Using **could** appropriately, talk about your abilities
that you have had but do not exist now.   Then using **could, couldn't, was able to,**
appropriately, talk about events and possibilities with your friends.

Unit 6   I might need to move out.

1 CONVERSATION

A Listen and practice. 🔊 CD-10

The following is a conversation between Yoko's landlord, Emily, and Yoko.
Listen to the conversation and answer the questions. Then practice the conversation with your partner.

Emily: Yoko!

Yoko: Yes!

Emily: Do you have time to talk with me for a minute?

Yoko: Yes, Emily.

Emily: I'd like to talk with you about a couple of problems. Would you not use the shower after 10 o'clock?

Yoko: 10 o'clock? Why not after 10?

Emily: Listen. You take a shower after midnight every day. We are sleeping. The sound of the shower wakes us up from our sleeping. It's noisy. Also, you use your dryer to style your hair for a long time after you take a shower.

Yoko: I'm sorry, but taking a shower before going to bed is a Japanese custom. I have to study hard until late at night for credits, or I will not graduate from my college.

Emily: I know you are studying hard every day. But you shouldn't bother us. Could you take a shower in the morning?

Yoko: In the morning? Take a shower in the morning? I can't! To be honest with you, I'm usually woken up by you when you take a shower in the morning. But I am patient. I don't complain about it.

Emily: People start to work in the morning. You might like to adjust yourself to our habits. Or you could take a shower before 10 o'clock and then you should resume your studies.

Yoko: Study again? How can I do that? People always go to bed right after showering in Japan.

Emily: Three people live in this house. You need to compromise for us in this house. One more thing. You take too much time to take a shower, almost 40 minutes. I don't charge you for that. I think it's a waste to use too much water. Could you finish it within 20 minutes?

Yoko: 20 minutes!? I need to shampoo my hair. Moreover, Japanese relax when we are taking a shower. We can't be in a hurry while we are taking a shower.

1. List the landlord's complaints against Yoko.

_____

_____

2. List the solutions so that the roommates in the house can compromise.

_____

_____

3. If you were Yoko, what would you do? Discuss about it with your partner.

_____

_____

B ▶ 💿 CD-11

Listen to the conversation below and answer the questions. Then practice the conversation with your partner.

Emily: It's smoky again. What are you cooking, Yoko?

Yoko: I'm cooking stir-fried vegetables. I need to eat vegetables here. I'm always eating junk food for lunch.

Emily: Isn't it better to use lower heat?

Yoko: No. Cooking with high heat is the most important point to make good stir-fried vegetables.

Emily: But it's too high, isn't it? It's so loud when you put the vegetables on the pan. The oil goes all around the stove.

Yoko: I'm sorry, but I always clean the kitchen after I use it.

Emily: But the oily smoke goes up to the ceiling and wall, and the room smells like oil. I think medium heat is enough.

Yoko: I always use the fan while I'm cooking. In addition, the vegetables become watery if I cook them with medium heat.

Emily: Yoko. Could you stop using the high heat in this house? I'm worried that my house will be greasy. I'm unhappy with this.

1. List Emily's complaints against Yoko with your partner. Then discuss the complaints. Why do they happen? What are the solutions?

2. Do you think that Yoko could stop using high heat? Discuss it with your partner.

3. Consider Yoko's situation in the conversation A and B. Then find out the best solution for her with your partner. Discuss the reasons.

4. If Yoko is going to move out, what do you advise her?

2 READING

Read Yoko's analysis, and then answer the questions below.

My landlord and my roommate are unhappy with me. Taking a shower before going to bed is a Japanese custom. This is the only time that I can relax here. This helps me study both mentally and physically. How can I change the time? How can I resume my study after taking a shower at 10:00? Taking a shower means bedtime for me, but Americans take a shower in the morning before they go to work. They finish their shower within 15 minutes. It's amazing to me. Americans use showers so differently than Japanese do.

Moreover, Emily is unhappy with me using high heat in the kitchen. I can't cook my favorite food correctly with low heat. Japanese people change the power of heat even within one cooking to make a delicious dish. I can't stop eating stir-fried vegetables here in America. This gives me energy both mentally and physically. My mother used to cook delicious stir-fried vegetables for us.

How can I live in this house without giving up my Japanese customs? Still, the cost of rent is reasonable here. Moreover, this house is close to school. I can't afford to pay more money for rent. I can't spend a lot of time to go to school. I have to economize money and time to pursue my studies. However, having living conditions that meet my style is important to me as well. After this semester, I need to find a different house. For now, I have to compromise with my roommates while I am in this house. I shouldn't bother them.

Question 1. What does taking a shower mean to Yoko?

Question 2. Why are Yoko's roommates unhappy with her taking a shower after she studies?

Question 3. When do Americans take a shower?

Question 4. List the positive aspects of Yoko's living in this house.

Question 5. Discuss the reasons why Yoko will not look for a new house now.

Question 6. How do you think Yoko will compromise to live in this house for now?

③ GRAMMAR FOCUS

People use **should** to give advice.

Give some advice to your friends, who are going to live in America, so that they are happy in the society.

1. _You should respect the people in speech and attitude._

2. _____

3. _____

4. _____

5. _____

Unit 7 — I want to make sure that I can take a shower after midnight.

1 CONVERSATION

A 🎧 CD-12

Listen to the conversation and then answer the questions.

Yoko: Is this Mrs.Barestrieri's house?

Mary: Yes, that's me.

Yoko: I saw your advertisement at school. You are looking for a roommate, right?

Mary: Yes.

Yoko: My name is Yoko Sato, a Japanese student. It's nice to meet you.

Mary: It's nice to meet you, too. Please, come in.

You have to respect this house.

Yes, I will.

****

Mary: I live in this house alone. My husband passed away 10 years ago. Now I'm 78 years old. I'd like to have a roommate.

Yoko: Really? I have been looking for a house to share. It's written that the rent is $300. Does that price include the utilities, too?

Mary: Yes, it does. I won't charge you any extra money except for your long distance calls. The rent is the same all year.

Yoko: I see. I have a couple of questions.

Mary: Sure, please ask away.

Yoko: I want to make sure: can I take a shower after midnight in this house? I am Japanese. We shower at night before we go to bed. Since I have to study hard here to take credits, I take a shower after midnight every day. Is it possible in this house?

Mary: Sure. No problem. My room is located on the other side of the bathroom. Your taking a shower won't bother my sleeping.

Yoko: I have one more question. Can I use your kitchen?

Mary: Of course. We share the kitchen.

Yoko: Can I cook my Japanese food?

Mary: Sure. No problem. I can't see why that would be a problem.

Yoko: Can I cook with high heat? I know that Americans usually don't use high heat, but I love stir-fried vegetables. I need to cook them with high heat. It doesn't take time, just a couple of minutes, but definitely with high heat. Or it becomes watery and doesn't taste good.

Mary: You can use high heat, but could you always keep our kitchen clean?

Yoko: Definitely. I will.

Mary: I know that Japanese people are polite.

Yoko: Thank you. I'd like to move into your house. Can I sign a contract with you now?

Mary: Sure, but I'd like to make one thing clear. You have to respect this house.

Yoko: Yes, I will.

Mary: Thank you. You need to pay one month's rent as a deposit and the rent for next month now. I'll return the deposit to you when you move out.

Yoko: I see.

Mary: You have to notify me about your moving one month ahead of the time. Or I can't return the deposit to you. All right?

Yoko: Sure. I understand.

Mary: Good. A student visited me before. She was interested in moving in to my house, but she left without paying me the deposit. First come, first served. You've had the priority to move into my house.

Yoko: Hmm, I think I will be happy in this house!

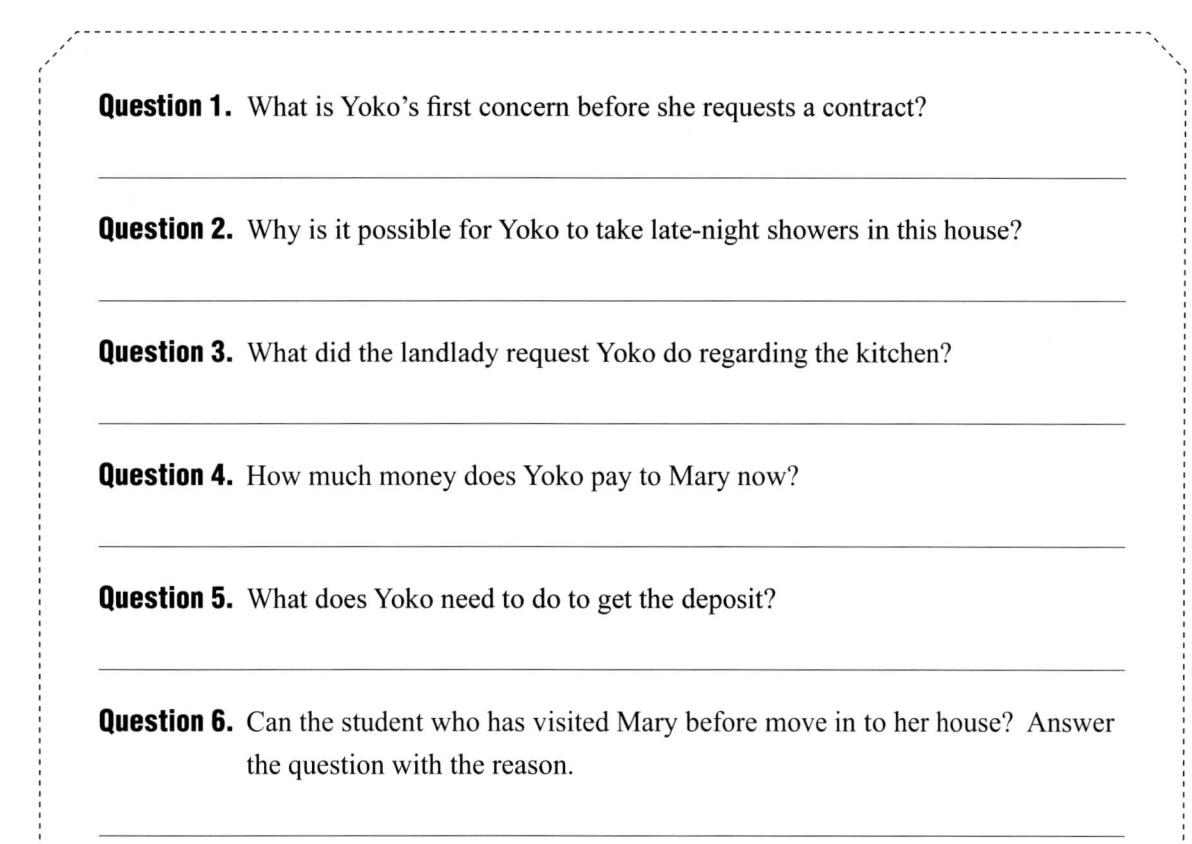

Question 1. What is Yoko's first concern before she requests a contract?

_____

Question 2. Why is it possible for Yoko to take late-night showers in this house?

_____

Question 3. What did the landlady request Yoko do regarding the kitchen?

_____

Question 4. How much money does Yoko pay to Mary now?

_____

Question 5. What does Yoko need to do to get the deposit?

_____

Question 6. Can the student who has visited Mary before move in to her house? Answer the question with the reason.

_____

B

Listen and practice the above conversation.

Sharing a house with roommates.

When you study abroad, it is important to make your living situation meet your needs. This will facilitate your studies. First of all, your house needs to be in a convenient location to access the school, library, and shopping mall. Second, even in different countries, people want to keep their own customs, habits, and foods. Since improving your target language is also the main purpose of your studies, you need to put yourself such situations where you can communicate with people who speak your target language. Having roommates, you can not only improve your English, but also experience different cultures, make foreign friends, and educate yourself to be capable of dealing with global issues.

Living in a different culture far from home is not easy, but it is a valuable and interesting experience. When people from different cultures live together, it is common for arguments to occur among them. For example, a Japanese person taking a shower late at night disturbs others while sleeping. The following day, it is sure that roommates will complain to the Japanese person. However, when others take a shower in the morning, it might bother the Japanese person's sleep. No Japanese person wants to be woken up by such a sound. In a house, arguments start among roommates. People in the house need to figure out some solutions, or people will be bothered with each other every day, and arguments will never end. This is because both the Japanese and their roommates hardly change their own customs concerning the time they take a shower.

Conflicts among people also happen in the kitchen. Eating good food supports students' health and energy for their studies. When I lived in the Midwest in the United States, I was eating meat and dairy products for protein every day. As a Japanese, I wondered if I damaged my health. One day my Japanese friend gave me a ride to a big market. Finding frozen sardines, I bought some immediately. I was delighted because I knew I could keep myself healthy by eating sardines. Sardines are the healthiest source of protein and it is healthy for the blood. As soon as I defrosted them in the microwave for my supper at home, I heard people in the house start to make a ruckus and then the door opened. Soon, my roommate came to the kitchen with a lit candle and said, "What are you doing!? It smells so bad!! My friends left!!! I had to light a candle!" I said, "I'm sorry, but these are American fish, not Japanese one. I need to eat fish here to keep myself healthy. I have been eating meat every day. We, Japanese people, need to eat fish." At the same time, in my heart, I realized that she and her friends couldn't tolerate the smell of my fish, and that was why she lit a candle to get rid of the bad smell. I also worried that her friends would never visit her at the house where a strange Japanese student had made a bad smell in the kitchen. I recognized that I should avoid doing what bothers people and decided not to cook frozen sardines in that house. I knew that I would be able to survive without eating sardines.

To be truthful, I didn't want to lose my roommates. Having nice roommates was fun. Moreover, I was able to save lots of money every month because I shared the rent with my roommates. If I had spent all my money, I would have had to go back home without having a degree. Furthermore, my roommates helped me by checking my homework before I handed it in to my teachers. I really benefitted from a native speaker's help with my papers. They were studying architecture, a major where only smart students were admitted, and I definitely needed their help in English.

In addition, we found new joy in the kitchen sharing food from our different cultures. One of my roommates loved my *oshiruko*, a Japanese sweet, made with mashed steamed sweet rice and red beans. Usually Americans don't like sticky and chewy food made from rice, but she loved it. I was happy to see my roommate enjoying my food.

When I saw one of my American roommates was making a cake, I recognized that she really came from a culture that uses wheat in its dishes. The process of baking a cake looked easy and simple for me, like our washing rice and make *gohan*, steamed rice. I learned about and enjoyed different cultures in the kitchen. Sharing a house and experiencing each other's cultures and food brought us closer together and made us friends.

In general, people don't want to have arguments with their roommates. However, we need to argue because we don't want to become victims of our roommates' behaviors. In fact, we should find ways to make our lives together comfortable. The common Japanese attitude of patience doesn't bring good solutions for people from different cultures. Rather this only worsens the problem. While we are patient, we are unhappy. The best solution is to talk about problems with our roommates. Listening to their opposite point of view, we need to speak our view to our roommate to find out the solution. We need to ask: "What's the problem?" Why do people need to be like that? When talking about a problem, some might feel that the problem is a small thing. On the other hand, people might discover that the problem is serious. If you recognize that the problem is serious and cannot be fixed to your acceptance, you should plan to move out to find a more agreeable living situation.

Having arguments with roommates in the same house isn't necessarily a negative thing. Rather it becomes the chance to improve English because people need both formal instructions in classes and communication with people outside of classes to acquire their target languages. Using vocabulary, expressions, and grammar that they have studied, people from different countries and cultures enthusiastically discuss things and even argue in English. Otherwise, they have to live in unhappy conditions because of different strange behaviors and customs in the house. They need to create sentences that express their view and persuade their roommates. Real communication happens while they are arguing. Moreover, the creativity of using language is one of the major elements to improve language skills. Indeed, my Japanese friend told me that having arguments with her roommate had become the first step to improving her English in the United States.

In addition, the process of people having arguments with people from different culture, finding a solution, and making decisions for a better future educates everyone in ways that are beneficial now and in the future. People worldwide need the knowledge to deal with global issues to solve problems. Young people in Japan hardly get such education in their home country where people mostly belong to the same culture and value the same things. All experiences while they are studying oversees are very valuable, even having arguments to find better solutions.

When you study overseas, I definitely recommend that you have roommates. When people from different cultures help each other and meet various situations in the house, they develop themselves as talented young people who can deal with diverse situations appropriately. As a result, you could grow up as a young person with skills all the world needs after you graduate from college.

A

List some important points when looking for a living situation and describe the reasons for each.

1. *To find a house close to school, library, and mall and that meets your budget.*

Reason: *students shouldn't waste time and money.*

2. _____

Reason: _____

3. _____

Reason: _____

Reason: _____

B

Tell the main reason that students from different countries argue.

_____

_____

C

Are there some positive aspects of having arguments in the house? If so, list the reasons.

1. _____

2. _____

_____

D

Tell the reason that the author stopped eating sardines.

_____

_____

E

List the positive aspects of having roommate.

1. *Minimize the cost of rent.*

2. _____

3. _____

4. _____

5. _____

F

What does the author say about the Japanese common solution, being patient?

G

If you were in the author's situation in a house and experienced problems with your roommate, what would you do? Discuss in your class.

Present perfect

Read the following conversations and think of the length of time that each person is talking about.

Mary: **I have been** living in this house alone. I'd like to have a roommate in this house.

Yoko: Really? **I have been** looking for a house.

Present perfect covers the length of time **from** some time in the past **to** now.

Pair work

Using present perfect, have conversations with your partner in the following situations.

a. It's around noon. You'd like to have lunch with your friend.

A: **Have** you **had** lunch yet?
B: No, not yet.
A: Why don't we have lunch at the cafeteria?
B: Sure. Let's go.

b. You'd like to visit London with your friend.
Expected sentence:

B: Have you been to London?
A:
B:
A:

c. You'd like to ask your American friend if she or he is interested in eating sashimi.
Expected sentence:

A: Have you tried sashimi?
B:
A:
B:

d. You can't improve your English despite studying in the United States for two years.

e. The pain in your stomach started two days ago. You need to explain it to your doctor.

1 WORD POWER 🔘 CD-13

Listening to each word or phrase, fill in each blank with the number appropriately.

1. headlight   **2.** tail light   **3.** side mirror   **4.** windshield wiper
5. rear window   **6.** steering wheel **7.** hood   **8.** rearview mirror
9. windshield   **10.** directional light **11.** wheel

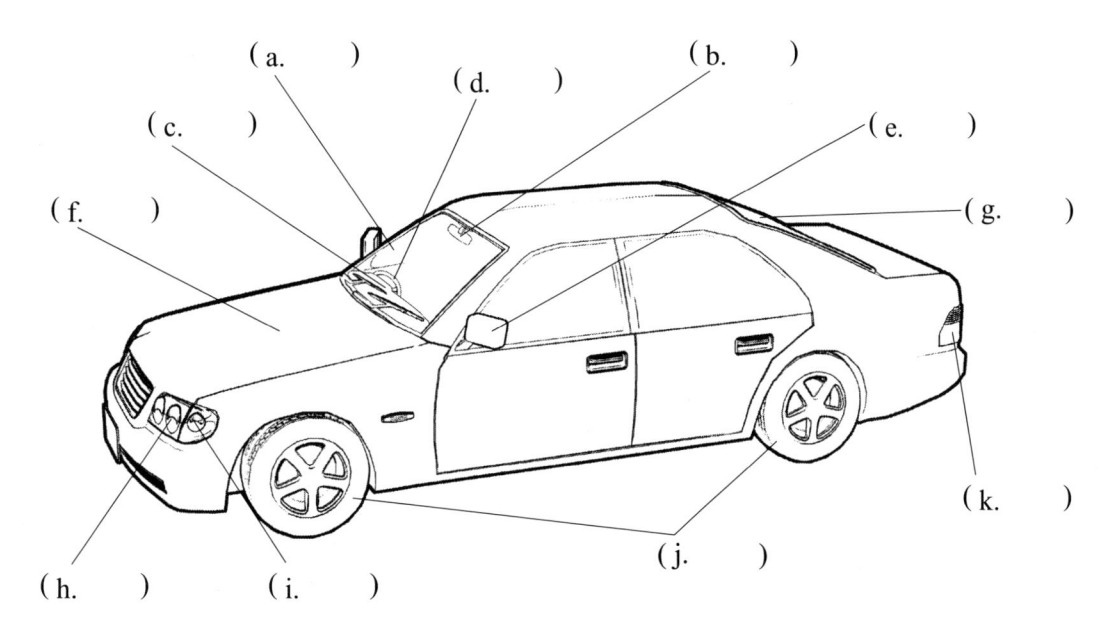

2 LISTENING

A 🔘 CD-14

Listen to the following conversation. Then answer the questions.

As Japanese people know, drivers in America drive on the right side and people walk on the left side of the road.

At a driving test

Inspector: Now we are going to an intersection. Turn left over there.
　Yoko: Sure. Turn left over there. The traffic signal is green. All right. Go.
Inspector: Stop!! Stop!! You'll kill us!! Stop!!

Question 1. Imagine what happened. Why did the inspector say like that?

_____

Question 2. What did Yoko do wrong? How should she have driven?

_____

Question 3. Why did she drive like that to turn left when the traffic signal was green?

_____

_____

_____

B

LISTENING
Vocabulary work

Match the word and the definition.

1. pedestrian	**a.** to stop a car to the side of a road
2. pull over	**b.** to join buckles together
3. fine	**c.** to allow other traffic to go first
4. yield	**d.** someone who is walking on a street
5. fasten	**e.** the money that someone pays as a punishment

 CD-15

Listen to the following conversation and answer the questions.

Yoko: So Evan, while we are driving, can you teach me about driving in the United States?
Evan: Sure.
Yoko: As you know, I failed the test for a driving license here. I think I need to become familiar with driving in America.
Evan: All right. We should drive somewhere.
Yoko: All right.
Evan: First of all, you need to fasten your seat belt.
Yoko: All right.
   (They begin driving)

Evan: Look, a school bus is stopping over there. You must never pass it while it is letting people out. You must stop and wait until it starts.

Yoko: All right.

Evan: It is against the law to pass a stopped school bus. If you pass a stopped school bus, you are subject to pay a fine.

Yoko: I see. Here, the children are really protected.

Evan: Yes, definitely. You never pass a school bus even if it is moving and there are two lanes. So you should turn right over there. We should drive on a different road.

Yoko: All right. But the traffic signal is red. I need to wait for the light to turn green.

Evan: No, you don't have to. For most red lights, after you stop, you can turn right if it is safe.

Yoko: What?

Evan: But you need to stop first, make sure if it is safe. And then turn right.

Yoko: Amazing! We never drive when the signal is red. It's illegal in Japan! Oh, I'm in the United States. The decision is made by each individual's responsibility, right?

Evan: Yes. But watch out! Pedestrians are walking on the sidewalk. You must yield the right of way to them, or you are charged a fine.

Yoko: Sure.

Evan: Now, go straight.

Yoko: All right, but, Evan, I hear a siren sound. What does that mean?

Evan: Yes, something must have happened on the street. We need to pull over when a vehicle with a siren, like a police car or fire truck, passes.

Yoko: Pull over? O.K. I will.

Question 1. List two things which impressed Yoko while she was driving.

1. _____

2. _____

Talk about the issues with your partner.

Driving in Vermont.

Foreigners who work, study, and live in America should definitely have some experience driving in the country. Going for a drive in America reminds people how comfortable American life can be and how big the country is. And they also see diverse cultures and enjoy beautiful scenery different from their home countries. Driving also makes people refreshed and gives them energy to pursue their work in this country. In Vermont, drivers will notice that the infrastructure has been well planned, and, therefore, the richness and beauty of nature has been maintained. Modern life is now rooted in nature.

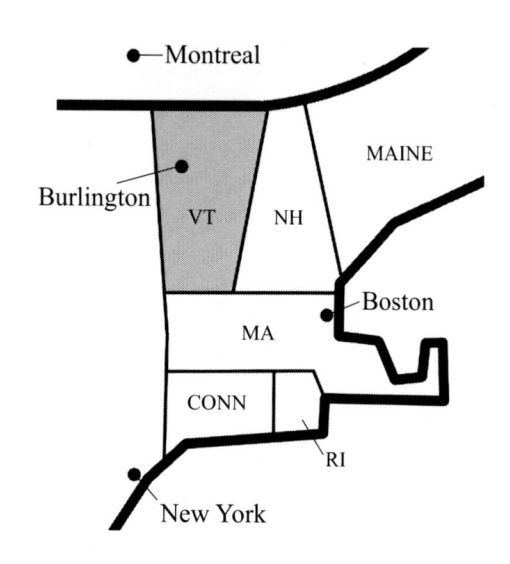

Geographically, the Canadian border is north of Vermont. It takes one and a half hours to drive from Burlington to Montreal, and three and a half hours drive to Boston, which is south of Vermont. The literal meaning of Vermont in French is "Green Mountain." The geographically rich nature provides people with good ski slopes and beautiful scenery every season. Since the quality of the snow is extremely good, people all over the United States and foreign countries visit Vermont to enjoy the winter sports, especially skiing.

Although winter in Vermont is long and there is a lot of snow-fall, life is very comfortable. The reason is that the people in Vermont can equally get snow plowed four times a day, six o' clock and twelve o'clock, as long as there is a public road and a person lives there, even in the mountain areas. This is guaranteed by the state law. Therefore, no one sees the hard winter season as the time of hardship. Negative words against the snow-fall are never heard there. When snow starts to fall, people, even though elderly people, are delighted.

However, drivers need to prepare their cars for the winter season. First, they have to get snow tires put on all four wheels early. Then change the fluid to antifreeze. They should keep a windshield scraper, a shovel, and at least a half tank of gas in their cars. Since doors are often frozen, drivers always need to have a lighter to defrost the ice and open them.

As roads can be icy and slippery, drivers need to lower their speed, be cautious when driving, and take more time to reach their destinations. Drivers should avoid braking suddenly and keep their car under control. Following these basic rules, they can enjoy winter driving since the roads are well plowed in Vermont.

By the way, some readers might have seen the movie, The Bridges of Madison County. The love story starts with a memo put at the entrance of a covered bridge in Iowa. There are more than one hundred covered bridges in Vermont. Quite a few of them were built in nineteenth century. The old wooden bridges are well suited to the landscape with pastures, meadows, and apple orchards. They create a special scene. Covered bridges are not in a museum, they are still in regular use. People drive through the covered bridges to cross rivers every day. They are never changed to concrete. In past, lovers waited at some covered bridges for their boyfriend or girlfriend. Also, people put post boxes at some bridges. The covered bridges are a dear source of beauty and fond memories in Vermont.

In fall, the sightseeing of covered bridges is highly recommended. As soon as the sugar maples start to change color to brilliant red, all of the green mountains are covered with gorgeous foliage. The best time to see it is from the end of September to around October tenth, quite a short period. As people drive through the foliage, they see a wooden bridge by a small village. This is "the essence of Vermont's special world" (Discover Vermont *Map & Guide*).

In Vermont, drivers should be cautious of animals that might be on the roadway especially in the evening and early morning. When drivers see that animals are roaming, they should reduce their speed and drive slowly so as not to scare the animals. Never honk, and avoid any actions that might startle animals. "Moose and deer are big animals, so a collision with them might cause a fatal accident for both the animals and the driver" (Ide, Shumlin & Searles 2013: 47).

As foreigners drive in Vermont, they are satisfied with the beautiful scenery. They realize that the people in Vermont have utilized the nature as a resource for the tourism industry without destroying it. Moreover, drivers are impressed at people's comfortable lives, even with modern buildings and industries exist in harmony with nature. They see here in Vermont, modernity makes the nature and beauty rich, and both nature and the modern life coexist.

Question

a. List some aspects of Vermont that attract visitors.

_____

b. Why do people in Vermont never say negative words in spite of their having a lot of snow-fall in winter?

_____

_____

c. List what drivers have to do to keep safe while driving in the winter in Vermont.

1. _____

2. _____

3. _____

4. _____

d. Why do you think people in Vermont never change the old wooden covered bridges to concrete ones?

_____

e. How should drivers drive when they see animals?

_____

4 GRAMMAR FOCUS

The use of much

Read following sentences, and then put a circle in each parenthesis if the sentence is grammatically correct. If a sentence is grammatically incorrect, correct the underlined part appropriately.

1. The people in Vermont have <u>much</u> snow in winter.   (   )

2. However, people don't have <u>much</u> snow fall this year.   (   )

3. I have a little money, but one of my friends, Nancy, is very rich. She has <u>much</u> money. (   )

4. The people of Florida have <u>much</u> sunshine all year.   (   )

5. I love rice. I eat <u>a lot of</u> rice.   (   )

6. You love sushi, but you eat too <u>much</u>. I worry you might get a stomachache.   (   )

> Explanation: **much** is used to show quantity with noncountable nouns only in negative sentences not affirmative sentence. People use **a lot of** in affirmative sentences. Concerning 6, the sentence, "you eat too much" looks like an affirmative sentence in surface. However, the sentence shows negative meaning. Therefore, the sentence is grammatically correct.

References

Azar, Betty Schrampfer (1989). <u>UNDERSTANDING AND USING ENGLISH GRAMMR.</u> New Jersey: Prentice-Hall, Inc.

Ide, Robert, Peter Shumlin & Brian Searles (2013). <u>VERMONT DRIVER'S MANUAL.</u> Vermont: Department of motor vehicles, Department of health.

Kawai, Tomoyuki (2015). *<u>オバマケア補助金支給は合法、米最高裁　大統領「勤労者の勝利」 www.nikkei.com/article/DGXLASGM25H83-V20C15A6FF2000/.</u> Tokyo: 日本経済新聞

Vermont Dept. of Travel & Tourism. <u>Discover Vermont *Map & Guide.*</u>

*American Supreme Court judged Government's subsidy for Obama Care to be legal. President says, "It's people's victory." Nikkei newspaper.

Answers:

Unit 1. Could you smoke in a smoking area?

1.CONVERSATION

A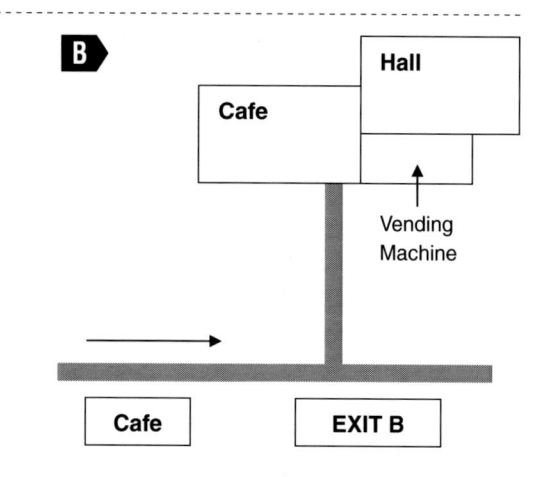

Question 1. At a cafe at an airport in America
Question 2. No, definitely not
Question 3. Smoking is not allowed here.
Question 4. The people, habits, laws, manners, and cultures

2.GRAMMAR FOCUS

a. Excuse me. Could you tell me where the shopping mall is?
b. Excuse me. Could you turn down your TV?
c. Excuse me. Could you give me a ride?
d. Excuse me. Could you pass the salad to me?

3.READING

A

1. e   **2.** d   **3.** a   **4.** c   **5.** b

B

1. to use acceptable words, especially concerning racial issues
2. to respect people and their diverse backgrounds

Unit 2. I'd like to open an account here.

1.WORD POWER

a. 3   **b.** 5   **c.** 4   **d.** 7   **e.** 2   **f.** 6   **g.** 1

2.CONVERSATION

A

Question 1: at a bank in the US
Question 2: her passport
Question 3: $50 by traveler's check
Question 4: her statement

Question 5: She can use it to make payment.

3. READING

a. 3 **b.** 2 **c.** 1

1. You need to understand the content of the document.

2. Concerning payments, you need to make sure who you are going to pay money to and the amount.

4. GRAMMAR FOCUS

Answers vary.

Unit 3. International students need to attend orientation.

1. WORD POWER

1. administration office **2.** semesters **3.** credits **4.** tuition

2. LISTENING

Question 1. The administration office

Question 2. Her passport and the document that Pauline sent to her

Question 3. It is a card issued by the university to students and it identifies who a student is.

Question 4. Willers Hall/ international students/ expected answers are: international students need some basic information that will facilitate their living and studies, and will help them avoid problems and crimes in the United States.

Question 5. She worries if she will be able to understand the teachers' lectures.

Question 6. No, they can't.

Question 7. Her view is that taking the English classes will help her study in classes at the college and will make her feel comfortable with her studies. She advised Yoko to talk about it with her adviser.

Question 8. Meets with her adviser, goes to registrar's office, and attends the orientation

3. READING

Question 1. Answers vary.

Question 2. Expected answer is: there is a curfew and strict rules in dorms in Japan, so they feel that their children's behavior is controlled by the college.

Question 3. Students themselves

Question 4. Answers vary

Question 5. Answers vary.

Question 6. Answers vary.

Question 7. Expected answers: People under the age of 21 must not drink alcoholic beverages. Men have to keep in mind that laws in some states protect women who have consumed alcohol and women have a right to sue a man after having dated.

4. GRAMMAR FOCUS

1. the   **2.** a. the. the

Unit 4. Could you clean the kitchen after you cook?

1.CONVERSATION

A

Question 1. Expected answers
> 1. Because their landlady always tells Yoko to clean the kitchen, and she thinks that Yoko leaves the kitchen messy.
> 2. Three people are sharing a kitchen, so she thinks that each person should clean the kitchen after she or he uses it for next person.

Question 2. Because Yoko told him that he must clean the kitchen.

Question 3. People do not use the auxiliary verb, must, in daily conversations in American English. She used it based on the translation from Japanese to English as she learned in her schooldays in Japan.

Question 4. 1. Could you clean the kitchen after you use it?
> 2. Can I ask you to clean the kitchen after you use it?
> 3. You need to clean the kitchen after you use it. ("have to" is also acceptable.)

2.READING

Question 1. Learners memorize the meaning of vocabulary through translation and then they translate sentences based on the grammar rule.

Question 2. People used the method to learn Latin.

Question 3. She thought that it is common sense to clean the kitchen after people use it. She translated the Japanese expression, *nebanaranai*, to English, *must*.

Question 4. She should have been taught the appropriate contexts that the auxiliary, must, is used and had the practice in communication.

3. GRAMMAR FOCUS

A

a. (a)   **b.** (i) need to/have to/should   **c.** (a)   **d.** (a)   **e.** (a)
f. (i) should/need to/have to   **g.** (a)   **h.** (i) should

B

(example answers)
a. You must not smoke here.
b. Children don't have to go to school on Sunday.
   Children don't have to pay the tuition for their compulsory educations at public schools.

c. Children need to go to bed at 8:00.

Children need to be disciplined to go to bed at 8:00.

d. Parents must take care of their children.

e. I have to eat vegetables to be healthy.

f. The pharmacist said, "You must take two pills after each meal".

The speaker is angry with the smoker.

Unit 5. Can I make an appointment with a doctor?

1.CONVERSATION

Question 1. Because Yoko didn't talk about her medical insurance.

Question 2. She has medical insurance issued in Japan.

Question 3. In general, Japan and the Japanese people are trusted among Americans, so is the medical insurance issued in Japan.

What seems to be your problem?

1. e   **2.** a   **3.** d   **4.** c   **5.** b

Question1. Fever, headache, cough

Question2. 38.3 degree Celsius

Question3. Prescribe medicine for her

Question4. Because there is no medicine for a cold

Question5. 1. Wash hands: to get rid of the germs

2. take shower: to accelerate the metabolism of her body

3. eat soup: to ease throat and nose with the moisture

4. drink orange juice: liquid and vitamin C

5. get some rest: to allow her body to recover

2. WORD POWER

a. 2   **b.** 3   **c.** 6   **d.** 7   **e.** 1   **f.** 4   **g.** 5   **h.** 8

B

1. b   **2.** c   **3.** g   **4.** h   **5.** a   **6.** f   **7.** d   **8.** e   **9.** i   **10.** j

C

a.   1. swollen   2. appetite

b.   3. allergic   4. sneezing

c.   5. vomiting   6. diarrhea

d.   7. infectious

3. ROLE PLAY

A

B

Refer the conversations of 1 B.

C

Create conversations by yourselves.

Doctor: What seems to be the problem?

Patient: I have a headache.

Doctor:

4. READING

A

a. 4   **b.** 5   **c.** 5   **d.** 2   **e.** 1   **f.** 7

B

1. Because poor people cannot afford to buy medical insurance
2. Because the cost is so high, insurance companies try to minimize costs.
3. Because doctors need to change medical treatments based on the type of insurance that patients have.
4. Supporting themselves even in medical matters is American tradition. / People feel government establishing medical insurance is intervention. / People are afraid of paying more money for medical insurances.
5. Insurance companies compensate for only that amount of time.
6. The medical cost is not high in the U.S since the insurance in Japan does not cover the treatment that she needs. / The medical fee in the U.S was cheaper because the value of the ¥ was high./She was able to get better treatment there than in Japan.
7. Because people who had problems speaking English went to America when $ 1 was worth 360 yen and had problems.

5. GRAMMAR FOCUS

A

1. past   (c)   4. past   (c)
2. past   (i)   5. future   (c)
3. past   (c)   6. present   (c)

B

1. (can't) (can't) (could)
2. (was able to) (could)

Unit 6. I might need to move out.

1.CONVERSATION

 A

1. Yoko's taking showers late at night bothers her roommates' sleeping.
   Yoko takes too much time in the shower.
2. Yoko takes shower in the morning or before 10 o'clock at night.
   Yoko should finish her taking shower within 20 minutes.
3. Answers will vary.

B

1. The answers vary. One of the answers might be that Yoko's cooking lowers the value of the house when Emily sells it.
2. Answers will vary.
3. Answers vary.
4. Answers vary. Expected answer is that she needs to talk about her use of bath room and kitchen before she has a contract.

2. READING

Question 1. It means relaxation for bedtime.
Question 2. This bothers them while they are sleeping.
Question 3. In the morning before going to work
Question 4. The rent is reasonable/ the location is close to her school
Question 5. She has to study hard, so she doesn't have time.
Question 6. Possible answers: she will take a shower before her roommates go to bed and use medium heat to cook stir-fried vegetables.

3. GRAMMAR FOCUS

Expected answers:
1. You should respect the people in speech and attitude.
2. You should use the shower before 10 o'clock.
3. You should be careful not to make too much smoke when you cook.
4. You should compromise with your housemates.
5. You should understand the culture of the country you are visiting.

Unit 7. I want to make sure that I can take a shower after midnight.

1.CONVERSATION

A

Question 1. She makes sure the rent includes the cost of utilities.
Question 2. Because the landlady's room is on the other side of the bathroom.
Question 3. Yoko needs to always keep the kitchen clean.

Question 4. $600

Question 5. She needs to tell Mary about her moving out one month ahead of the time.

Question 6. No, she can't because she didn't sign a contract with Mary.

2. READING

A

1. To find a house close to school, library, and mall and that meets your budget.
   Reason: students shouldn't waste time and money.
2. To find a house where one can keep those parts of culture that are necessary to feel comfortable and happy.
   Reason: studying doesn't go well without it.
3. To find a house with roommates
   Reason: students improve their English by communicating with their roommates. Experiencing diverse situations, students educate themselves.

B

Different cultures clash because they have very different customs that are not in harmony.

C

1. Students can improve their English by having arguments.
2. Through finding solutions to arguments with students from different countries, everyone becomes an educated young person that the whole world needs.

D

She thought she shouldn't do what her roommates don't like.

E

1. Minimize the cost of rent.
2. Students improve their English by communicating with their roommates.
3. Learning and enjoying different cultures and foods, students in the house become friends.
4. Students learn that they shouldn't do what their roommates don't like.
5. Young people educate themselves as people that the world needs.

F

Being patient does not bring any solution, but causes unhappy situations to last longer.

G

Answers will vary.

3. GRAMMAR FOCUS

b. Expected sentence: Have you been to London? Conversations vary.

c. Expected sentence: Have you tried *sashimi*? Conversations vary.

d. Expected sentence: I have been studying in the United States for two years. Conversations vary.

e. I have been suffering for the stomachache for two days. Conversations vary.

Unit 8. Driving in Vermont.

1. WORD POWER

a. 9   **b.** 8   **c.** 4   **d.** 6   **e.** 3   **f.** 7   **g.** 5   **h.** 1   **i.** 10   **j.** 11   **k.** 2

2. LISTENING

A **At a driving test**

Question 1. Yoko drove to the middle of intersection to wait for oncoming traffic to pass.

Question 2. She should have waited at the white line until oncoming cars have passed.

Question 3. She drove to the middle of an intersection to yield oncoming cars as she turned right in Japan. This is the rule in Japan, but the same thing is against the traffic laws in the U.S.

B

LISTENING

Vocabulary work

1. d   **2.** a   **3.** e   **4.** c   **5.** b

Question 1.

1. Drivers must not pass a school bus.

2. Drivers can turn right after stopping, even though the traffic signal is red.

3. READING

a. Winter sports, beautiful scenery, foliage, the country life

b. Every person gets snow plowed four times a day on the road that his or her house faces, so the life is comfortable.

c. 1. Get snow tires put on all four wheels early.

2. Change the fluid to antifreeze.

3. Keep a windshield scraper, a shovel, a lighter, and half tank of gas in their cars.

4. Lower speed and avoid sudden brakes.

d. Old wooden bridges are suited to the nature and beautiful.

e. Drive slowly and avoid honking and any actions that startle them.

4. GRAMMAR FOCUS

1. a lot of   **4.** a lot of

2. ○   **5.** ○

3. a lot of   **6.** ○

Author's Profile

Kazuko Tanimich

University of Wisconsin-Milwaukee,
Bachelor of Arts-College of Letters and Science in
Linguistics, 1994
Saint Michael's College, Graduate School
Master of Arts Degree in Teaching English as a
Second Language, 1997
Formar lecturer of the University of Kanazawa

谷道 和子

学士号　ウイスコンシン大学人文学部言語学科
修士修了　セイントマイケルス　カレッジ大学院
第二言語としての英語教授法
元金沢大学講師

Living in the United States
Its language, culture, and customs

2018 年 6 月 1 日　初版発行

■ Author ——— Kazuko Tanimichi
■ Publisher ——— SANKEISHA Co,. Ltd
　　　　　　　　2-24-1 Chumaru-cyo Kita-Ku, Nagoya-City
　　　　　　　　462-0056, Japan
　　　　　　　　TEL 052-915-5211 FAX 052-915-5019
　　　　　　　　URL http://www.sankeisha.com

■ 著　者———谷道 和子
■ 発 行 所———株式会社　三恵社
　　　　　　　〒462-0056 愛知県名古屋市北区中丸町 2-24-1
　　　　　　　TEL 052-915-5211 FAX 052-915-5019
　　　　　　　URL http://www.sankeisha.com